Our Fairy Tale
Romance

Our Fairy Tale Romance

how I met a "princess in disguise" and convinced her to marry me

by andrew schmiedicke

CHESTERTON PRESS
FRONT ROYAL, VIRGINIA

Also from Chesterton Press:

The Fairy Tale Novels by Regina Doman

The Shadow of the Bear: A Fairy Tale Retold
Black as Night: A Fairy Tale Retold
Waking Rose: A Fairy Tale Retold
The Midnight Dancers: A Fairy Tale Retold

Text copyright 2009 by Andrew Schmiedicke
Cover design 2009 by Regina Doman

Chesterton Press
P.O. Box 949
Front Royal, VA 22630

www.chestertonpress.com

Summary: If you're a lonely Catholic bachelor stuck in a dead-end job, how can you find someone to marry? The author shares his experience of hardship, courtship, and marriage to the author Regina Doman in this inspirational booklet.

ISBN: 978-0-9819318-9-0
Printed in the United States of America

1

looking for life direction

At 25 years of age I was already a lonely bachelor. After a number of failed relationships in high school, college, and after college; after a number of journeys, adventures, and failed business and employment ventures; I found myself back in Michigan, looking for a job, and feeling…well…like a failure. And a bachelor.

After a period of profligacy during college, I had rediscovered the beauty and truth of my childhood faith and began practicing it again. Soon I was inspired like the knights of old to dedicate myself to the protection and defense of those who are most vulnerable; in this case, endangered babies and their mothers. Quests and missions ensued. Along the way I met several promising young ladies, yet I was still single.

And now I was unemployed, living in the cave-like basement of my parents' house, thinking of all the time and money I had spent on my bachelor's degree. Apparently the only result was that I was still a bachelor.

I prayed for my future spouse daily, particularly seeking the help of the Holy Family and St. Raphael the Archangel. Since he had arranged such a good marriage for Tobiah and Sarah as recorded in the Book of Tobit in the Bible, I figured he could help me find a good spouse too. But at the time I had no means of supporting a wife and children. I couldn't even support myself. Fortunately, St. Raphael was also the patron saint of finances, so I thought he could help me with that too.

> **Apparently the only result of my bachelor's degree was that I was still a bachelor.**

After two months of fruitlessly sending out resumes, I got a job. Well, actually, my Aunt Pati got me the job: a minimum wage job at a clothing store where she worked a couple hours away. Not exactly what I had hoped to get with a double major in Communication Arts and German, but it was better than feeling like a poor peasant in my parents' basement.

Three weeks later I got a better job back in my home town of Greenville working as a cashier in a lumberyard. It paid more than the clothing store. And I could move out of my parent's basement.

My Grandmother Kane offered to rent me a bedroom at her house, which was close to the lumberyard. In her generosity, she only charged me $25 a week in rent, and she let me know she was putting $15 of that rent into a savings account for me. Her kindness meant so much to me.

8

Yet I still felt like a serf. I worked at the lumberyard for a few months with my face feeling hot and my stomach filling with acid every time some former fellow high school classmate came into the store. I guess the fact that my dad was head of the English Department at the high school had something to do with that.

I could just imagine what they were thinking. *Soooo, you were one of the brighter kids in high school, your dad was head of the English Department, you went to college, got your degree and...decided...you really wanted to work as a cashier in a lumber yard. Oookay.* Awkward.

In the days leading up to my 26th birthday, I remember praying a special novena to know what God wanted me to do. On my birthday after work, I got a call from Tom Sayre, a lawyer friend of mine in West Virginia. He was opening an independent law office in a small town and he wanted to know if I would be interested in being his legal assistant. Boy, would I ever! Finally, something that sounded like a real job with growth potential. We made our final agreement on the last day of the novena.

I had a feeling that this time I'd be leaving home for good so I decided to ask my dad for his blessing before I ventured off into the world to seek my fortune.

I began to think seriously that perhaps God was calling me to the priesthood.

Early on the morning of my departure Dad and Mom met me at my grandmother's house, and I gave him the prayer I wanted him to pray. We went into the living room, and I knelt down while my dad prayed for me and gave me his blessing. I think my mom cried a little.

Glad for my father's blessing, I headed down to West Virginia with all my belongings in the back of my little Chevy S-10 pick-up truck. Life direction at last!

However, though I was happy enough with the job, it quickly became apparent to me that the chances of meeting a suitable spouse in such a tiny town tucked away in the tight hills of West Virginia were slim to none.

It turned out to be none.

After half a year or so of increasing loneliness and other difficulties, Tom and I came to a mutual decision that I should leave my position with his office. I began to think seriously that perhaps God was calling me to the priesthood. I made arrangements to accompany a group of Franciscan University of Steubenville students who were going to visit some friars. Life direction again?

At the end of January 1993, I left West Virginia and drove up to Steubenville, Ohio to meet the group. I spent the night with my sister's in-laws, the Nelson family. They said I could stay with them as long as I liked.

Before the group left, I stopped by to see my friend Mike Hernon. He was recently engaged to a girl named Alicia Doman. When I arrived, he asked if he could talk to me privately. So we went to a room where I sat down wearily from my travels, disappointments in my employment failures, lack of life direction, and loneliness.

"How you doing?" Mike asked cheerfully.

"Tired," I said. "I'm just really tired."

"Too tired to be my best man?" he asked with an Irish grin on his face.

I was surprised to tears, and choking a little, I said, "I could do that."

Later that evening we went to a "Festival of Praise" at the campus chapel. I again was thinking that perhaps God was calling me to be a priest. I looked forward to meeting the leader of the group that was going to visit the friars. I was ready to explore this new direction in my life.

So the next day, I met the group leader at morning Mass at St. Peter's church. After greeting her, I enthusiastically told her that I was all ready to go with them. There was a slight pained expression on her face. She explained that since I was new to the group and that there were already some internal conflicts she was trying to handle, she decided that it would be best if I didn't go with them after all.

"Oh." I said blinking and surprised. "OK. I understand. Well, thanks anyway," I said.

"Yeah. I'm sorry," she said.

I went back into the chapel, feeling as though the Lord had slammed a door in my face. "Well, Lord, now what do you want me to do?"

Maybe He wanted me to get married after all. "Good," I thought. "Because that's what I want too."

That evening, I told Mike Hernon of this latest event, and he suggested I talk with Alicia's sister, Regina. She worked as an assistant editor at *Lay Witness* in New York City and might know of a job opening there. Sounded good to me. So I spoke with Regina on the phone. She was friendly, but she didn't know of any openings. However, I could send my resume in case anything opened up. I did send my resume, but nothing ever came of it.

So I moved in with the Nelsons and got a handyman job with an old acquaintance. And I met with my spiritual director, Father Giles Dimock, O.P., about my vocation: priesthood or married life? He recommended I ask God for clarification about that on a retreat. I had scheduled a weekend retreat at the Holy Family Hermitage, a Camaldolese Monastery.

Father Giles counseled, "Try imagining yourself as a priest; then as a married man. Pay attention to what thoughts or feelings you experience during those imaginations."

I did that on the retreat. When I was alone in the small stone chapel, I approached the altar and imagined myself as a priest offering the Mass. I thought I would experience a rush of joy...But I didn't. I felt awkward and out of place.

> If God wanted me to marry, how was I to support a wife and family?

Then I imagined myself at Mass with my future wife and children by my side. I was filled with happiness and felt a strong desire to be with that woman who would be my wife. So I felt certain that this was the direction God was leading me in.

Thinking hard, I genuflected, left the chapel and returned to my retreat cell, pondering. How was I to support a wife and family? I couldn't exactly do it by just being a handyman. I had a desire to work in the church as a teacher of theology or a DRE, but I didn't have a degree in theology and I didn't have money to pay for — *Wait a minute! If the Nelsons really will let me stay with them free of charge as long as I need, I won't have to pay college room and board. And maybe I can get loans to cover the tuition. It just might work.*

I left the retreat with renewed hope.

Returning to Steubenville, I asked the Nelsons if I could continue to live at their home while I pursued a Master's Degree in Theology. They generously said I was welcome to. Then I spoke to an admissions counselor at FUS about student loans. He said that I could get loans to cover the entire tuition (about $30,000) for the three years needed to complete my M.A. I was so excited to finally have a clear direction for my life for the next few years, so I called my parents to tell them the good news. They were…less than enthused.

"We just don't want to see you go into that much debt, Andrew," my mom said in a pained and concerned voice.

"But Mom, I don't know what else to do. I feel like I'd finally have some direction in my life for the next few years and at the end of it have something I can turn into a career."

"I don't know, Andrew. $30,000 is just an awful lot of debt to be starting off in married life. Aren't there any scholarships or grants you could get?"

A bit deflated, I admitted, "The only one the counselor told me about was 'The Disciple of Christ' scholarship, but he said it's like finding a needle in a haystack."

"Well, try it anyway. We really don't want to see you go into that much debt."

"All right. I'll apply for that. If I don't get it, I won't pursue getting this M.A. degree," I promised my mom.

So I applied for the scholarship, writing the necessary essay. And then the weeks of waiting followed. I continued my handyman jobs and wondered what in the world I would do if I didn't get the scholarship. I tried to stay calm and detached about the outcome and trusting God's will. Some days I was confident that God would grant me the scholarship. Other days I wasn't so sure.

I remember one day in early May as I was working outside at my employer's house. It was a lovely day. The trees and grass were lush and green. There was dew on the grass and birds chirping merrily in the trees. The sky was blue and full of sunlight. But I...could not see. I worked mechanically

> **I tried to stay calm and detached about the outcome and trusting God's will, but it was tough.**

in silence. I had no foresight; no sense of whether God would grant me the scholarship or not.

One of my employer's housemates saw me. He came over to me and asked how I was doing.

I looked at him probably with a face devoid of any cheer or hope and said, "It's dark. It's all dark and I can't see." I was surrounded by a beautiful sunlit spring day, but interiorly, I was in utter gloom.

"You still haven't heard if you got the scholarship then?" he asked.

"No," I said.

"Well, you know what they say. It's always darkest before the dawn."

I tried hard to trust and to choose to be happy, even though my path ahead was still unknown to me. Within a couple of days, I found I could be cheerful while working.

Then, a day later, I got a phone call. As soon as I recognized the admissions counselor's voice, I knew I had gotten the scholarship. As he congratulated me on winning the Disciple of Christ scholarship, I felt a surge of joy knowing that I had a definite direction in my life, and new hope for my goal of being able to support a wife and family.

2

Bring the woman into my life, Lord!

Shortly after this I got a call from my lawyer friend in West Virginia asking if I could come back to work for him during the summer until classes began in the fall. Grateful for the chance of stable income to tide me over, I went back to work for him.

I was also reading a journal called *Caelum et Terra* and came across an article by Regina Doman titled, "The Church as One Big Rowdy Family", which I enjoyed. I submitted an article of my own to the journal, but ended up getting in a rather heated disagreement with the editor about it. I told Mike Hernon a little about the argument and he suggested I come up to Steubenville to talk with Regina about it since she personally knew the editor. She was leading a youth group to a FUS Youth Conference in July and I could meet with her then and discuss the situation.

So one hot, humid Saturday evening in July, I walked uphill to a huge red-and-white circus tent perched on a University soccer field where the Youth Conference was being held. Inside, thousands of young people were cheering, singing, and praising God. By now I was used to the "Steubenville milieu."

Mike led me to one corner beside the stage where a group of teens in light blue t-shirts were located. Their leader was a girl in a denim jumper and matching t-shirt with rather disheveled wavy brown hair. "This is Regina," Mike shouted (we could barely hear each other over the crowd). I said hi, and joined the group. I was wearing a white shirt and blue jeans that had faded to a very light, pale blue. Regina thought I was dressed all in white, and said to herself, "That guy doesn't know how to dress."

The priest who was speaking was asking all those who thought they might have a religious vocation to come forward for prayers, as well as those who thought God was calling them to ministry in the Church. Of course I knew I had to go forward. I wondered if I was resisting God's call. After all, a degree in theology would fit perfectly with the priestly vocation. Regina took note that I went forward for prayers.

The next day, after Sunday Mass, I met Mike and Alicia at the local Bob Evans for breakfast. Regina was there: again, she was dressed in the same blue denim jumper, but this time with a white t-shirt, and her hair was a little less messy. We exchanged pleasantries, but fairly quickly we started talking about *Caelum et Terra* and related issues.

Regina was very easy to talk to, but I didn't feel the slightest hint of a romantic interest. I found out she was living in a young adult's house run by the

Franciscan Friars of the Renewal in New York City. Perhaps that explained the plain dress.

She also said she had organized and brought up a group of thirty high school students from three states to the conference. In those days, the youth conferences were held completely in large tents: participants met and slept in tents all weekend. What Regina didn't tell me was that, in coordinating

> **A**gain, I decided to look into pursuing the priesthood. I was still not at peace.

sleeping arrangements for all her teens, her own luggage had gone missing. She had been sleeping in the same clothes all weekend, except for borrowing a clean t-shirt to wear to our meeting. So I guess it's fair to say neither of us was looking our best during our first meeting.

I returned to West Virginia pondering and conflicted. Over the next couple of weeks or so a priest friend in West Virginia strongly encouraged me to consider the priesthood — despite me telling him of my desire for marriage. He said he thought I'd make a good priest. Feeling the pressure, I told him I'd think and pray about it. Maybe it was because of his influence that I decided to look into pursuing the priesthood again when I returned to FUS.

Shortly before classes began I made a private weekend retreat in the eastern hills of Ohio. I wanted to spiritually prepare for the three years of study ahead and seek God's will regarding my vocation. I was still not at peace about it.

જજ

Meanwhile, in August, Regina was on vacation with her family and family friends at Cape Hatteras, North Carolina. She was watching a father play with his young children. As she watched him she thought, "You know, I bet that guy, Andrew, would make a good dad."

Suddenly, Jane Robinson, a married friend of Regina's, looked at her and said, "Regina, who are thinking about right now?"

Regina blushed and said, "Just this guy I met."

The mother responded solemnly, "He's the one for you."

"What?! What do you mean? I just met him!"

"I don't know. I just know he's the one for you."

Not sure of what to think, Regina pondered this incident for a long time, especially in the light of subsequent events.

જજ

After my retreat, I met with my spiritual director, Father Giles, again and discussed with him my doubts about my vocation. He said, "Andrew, we've been discussing and praying about this for quite some time. It is clear to me that unless there is some extraordinary sign to the contrary, your vocation is marriage." That helped put me at peace.

Father Giles suggested I take a part-time job at the computer center on campus after I started classes. So I started a job I was to keep for the next three years, where I gained valuable job experience that led to my first salaried position after graduate school, as well as to my current career. Even though I didn't realize it at the time, the financial part of my vocation was falling into place.

But as for the marriage part—nothing. No wife, no fiancé, no girlfriend, no dates. My attempts to get to know some of the other Catholic girls on campus went nowhere.

Still, I was getting periodic phone calls from Regina regarding plans and events leading up to Mike and Alicia's wedding in January. Since Alicia was the first Doman child to be getting married, Regina and her family had planned some elaborate celebrations they wanted me to be a part of. I found that Regina, the oldest of ten, had a lot in common with me as the oldest of eleven children. We discovered that we both came from large and rather devout Catholic families. Our occasional conversations were pleasant, but didn't seem to go beyond that.

I was beginning to get frustrated in my search for a wife. What was particularly frustrating was that I was attending a Catholic university where there were so many vibrant and wonderful girls. Couldn't one of them be the one I was looking for? And yet, it seemed that the elusive "she" was nowhere to be found.

The week before Thanksgiving, I expressed my frustration to Father Giles. He told me to ask Jesus to bring the young woman into my life who was to be my wife. So I did. "Lord, if you want me to marry, bring the woman into my life!"

Yet it always seemed that the elusive "she" was nowhere to be found. I began to get frustrated.

And then I thought of Beth Morson, a young woman in town, with whom I'd been friends for a few years. I realized that she had many of the qualities I was looking for in a wife, and wondered if she might be the one. I arranged to meet her the last day of school before the Thanksgiving break.

But, as soon as I met with Beth and awkwardly asked her to consider the possibility of dating, I could tell it wasn't going to go anywhere, though Beth was kind enough to say she'd consider it.

I went away from the meeting disappointed.

I had been invited to spend the Thanksgiving break with the Doman family. Mike Hernon had invited me to drive to Pennsylvania with him and Alicia. I was glad for the invitation, but my melancholy mood was heightened during the six-hour drive. I had too much time to think, and it didn't help that Mike and Alicia, were in the front of the car holding hands, and Alicia's brother, Martin and his girlfriend Charlene were sitting in the back with me. Martin and Charlene snuggled and talked next to me while I stared out the window at the drab late fall scenery passing by, feeling like a fifth wheel.

"Well, maybe I'll meet a young lady on this trip who will turn out to be the one," I tried to think positively.

"Stop it, Andrew," another side of me said. "You always think *that* whenever you go on a trip, and it never works out. Just go there, meet the Domans, be pleasant, have a good time, and then just go back to your studies."

So I let go of my wishful thinking and mentally entrusted myself to Jesus and Mary.

3

I fall in love with the Doman family — and edit Regina's manuscript

On arriving at the Domans' house that night, Alicia, and Mike led the way into the kitchen where they were greeted with exuberant cheers, hugs, and kisses from Alicia's mom and dad, younger brothers and sisters, and especially a cute toddler with blond curls and a round cherub face named Anna. I was warmed and impressed by the outpouring of mutual love and affection — so much so that I began wondering how I could become part of this family.

I spent the first hour with fifteen-year old Johnny looking through a Tolkien Bestiary and discussing *The Lord of the Rings*.

The next day I had some papers to work on for my classes so Mrs. Doman set me up to work on their computer in their bedroom. A little while later two-year old Anna peered at me from the doorway. I looked over at her and smiled, then returned to typing. She toddled into the room, over to my chair and looked up at me. I looked down at her. She then proceeded to climb into my lap and sit there while I typed on the computer.

I was touched that she had such trust in me so soon. A few minutes later twelve-year old Maria came to the door and observed me. I looked over at her.

With a smile, she said, "Andrew, you're cool."

I laughed and asked, "Why do you think I'm cool?"

"I don't know," she shrugged. "I just think you're cool."

I was in love with this family.

⊱⊰

Later on, I was walking down the hallway where the Domans had dozens of framed family photos. One frame caught my eye: a large photograph of a lovely dark-haired young lady. The picture was hanging near photos of Alicia, Martin, and David— the older Doman children. I gazed at the picture of the young woman I didn't recognize and thought, "She is really lovely. I wonder who she is."

Was she perhaps an older sister I hadn't met or heard about yet? But no, I knew Regina was the oldest sister, and there weren't any sisters between her and Alicia. Was she perhaps a Doman cousin? But why would the Domans put a picture of a cousin with pictures of their eldest children? And not include their oldest daughter, Regina? That seemed odd. No, it couldn't be a cousin. I knew there were ten Doman children so I counted off the ones I had met. Finally, I looked at the picture and whispered, "Regina?"

She looked so different in the picture, like a princess: her dark hair was smooth and stylish, and she wore a dark blue dress and pearls. When I had met her in Steubenville, she had seemed more like a plain peasant girl. Was she a princess in disguise?

> When we met before, she had seemed more like a plain peasant girl. Was she a princess in disguise?

Finally, I pointed to the picture and casually asked Mike, "Is that Regina?"

"Yeah," he said.

"Oh," I said. "Uh—why doesn't she wear her hair like that anymore?"

"I don't know."

That evening Regina arrived from her job in New York. I wondered at the plainness of how she now dressed and carried herself. Was she deliberately trying to hide her beauty?

She brought with her the first draft of a manuscript she had been working on that past year, which she had just completed. After supper, Regina and her brother, John, who, I found out, was also a writer, were discussing the story at the dining room table.

I asked them what they were talking about, and Regina said it was a book she was working on, based on the Grimm's fairy tale called "Snow White and Rose Red."

"Oh, yeah," I said, recognizing the story.

"Not 'Snow White and the Seven Dwarfs'," she said with a sigh. "It's a different one."

"I know," I said. "'Snow White and Rose Red'. It's one of my favorite fairy tales."

"Really?" Regina asked, surprised. She had taken note that not only did I know the story but that I had listed it among my favorites and she therefore deduced that I was a person who, like herself, took fairy tales seriously. "Well, would you like to read my manuscript?"

"Sure," I said.

So I began reading the draft of the book that would one day become *The Shadow of the Bear: a Fairy Tale Retold*. It was very rough. I could tell that she was trying to be creative and descriptive in her narrative, but I thought it was rather overdone: "Mother, the strong: Mother, the pillar of strength..." But I knew how sensitive some people could be about their creative writing. Writing can be so personal because you pour your heart into it...and each red correction or critique mark on your paper is like blood oozing from your heart. So I held back.

27

Yet, as head of the high school English department, my dad had thoroughly instructed me in English grammar and literature for three years. I had even helped him correct the papers and tests of my classmates. And as I continued reading Regina's manuscript I began noticing mistakes in spelling and grammar which I could not pass over. I cautiously asked Regina for a pencil and made a couple of corrections.

"Hey, that's great," Regina said enthusiastically. "If there is anything else you see that could make it better, please let me know."

"OK," I said, feeling freer to tell her what I thought. "Well, I would get rid of all of this…" and I struck out several paragraphs with a diagonal line, "and all of this…" I removed several more. "I just don't think these kind of extended descriptions add anything to the story."

We continued working on her manuscript until after one in the morning.

I wondered if she would be angry, but instead she looked relieved and enthusiastic. "I was trying to decide if those parts should go," she said. "Wow, this is great! Most people just say to me, 'Looks good. Better than I could do.' Please, tell me what else should change."

So we went on reading and working together, removing wordy descriptions and repetitions so that the opening scene would flow better. Regina was delighted. We continued working on her manuscript until after one in the morning, both of us engrossed in the story. By the end of it I was sensing…something — I wasn't sure what — between us.

Just before she went to bed, Regina gave me a poem she had recently written about coming home for Thanksgiving. Then she left me in the kitchen reading it. It was a lovely poem, and once again I was struck by the beauty of something that this plainly-dressed girl had written. After she walked back down the hall to her room, I set the poem down, frowned, and said quietly, "God? What's going on here?"

4

I fall in love with Regina and decide I'm going to marry her — but I can't tell her that!

I went to bed perplexed, but woke up the next day, Thanksgiving Day, calm and at peace. I went to Mass with Regina, her parents, and Mike Hernon. Afterwards, Mike, Regina, and I went on various errands related to Mike's upcoming marriage to Alicia: the tuxedo place, the florists — not the most exciting places in the world, but it was fun to go along for the ride.

Back at the Domans' house there was all the hustle and bustle of preparing the Thanksgiving feast. I followed Regina around helping her with various tasks. I met Regina's tall, blond, and lovely cousin, Christine, who had come over to visit. I was informed that she was teaching English at a private Catholic high school. When she and Regina went for a walk in the back yard, I went with them. At dinner I was seated across from Christine. She was strikingly beautiful, but I felt more comfortable talking with Regina.

I think everyone was dying to find out what was going on between Regina and me. Later, I was to find out that every time I left a room, Regina's family and friends would rush over to her and frantically whisper, "What's going on with you two?" To which she responded, "I don't know. He hasn't said anything. He just keeps following me around."

> **I remember her dad watching us from the living room door and smiling.**

After dinner, Christine left, and I was sitting on the living room sofa, looking at books with Regina and John, sipping wine and nibbling on bits of homemade pumpkin and apple pies. Martin had put on some Harry Connick, Jr. jazz music and he and David were swing dancing with their respective girlfriends. I told Regina, "I know we have to dance at Mike and Alicia's wedding since we're in the wedding party, but I don't know how to dance."

"Oh, my brothers can teach you," Regina said.

"Yeah, we can teach you," said Martin and David.

So with Regina as my partner, David and Martin taught me some basic swing dance steps to Harry Connick, Jr.'s "It Had to Be You." I was thoroughly delighted. One might say "euphoric." I remember Regina's dad watching us from the living room door and smiling. Was it a knowing smile?

At the end of our last practice dance for the night, Regina and I, probably feeling a little giddy, gave each other a side hug. And smiling down at her, I suddenly knew.

Jesus, I'm falling in love with her. That's what's going on! I'm falling in love with her! I'm sure a big goofy grin broke out on my face at these thoughts.

Sure, in my past I had thought that I was "in love" with girls I was dating, but this was different. This time, I felt both calm and confident: I felt a deep sense of peace while bubbling over with joy. And there was this sense of knowing. I didn't just think I knew. I *knew* that I knew.

Regina was smiling up at me, a little surprised (she knew something was up but didn't know what). And Regina's dad was still smiling at us from the doorway.

He knows, I thought. And as I walked passed him to go down to the basement to sleep, he pulled me into a manly hug and said, "Andrew, I just want you to know we're all so glad you came to spend Thanksgiving with us."

Yup. He knows, I thought. I smiled. Out loud I said, "Thank you. I'm glad I came too."

As I was going down the stairs I was thinking, *I'm in love with her. That's what's going on. I'm in love with her.*

Some months later I was to learn that as I was walking down stairs in exhilaration, Regina was walking upstairs thinking to herself rather disappointedly, *He can't dance.*

Downstairs, I got ready for bed, talking excitedly in my head to our Lord. *Jesus, that's what's been going on. I've been falling in love with her. I'm going to marry her.* And then I thought, *Wait a minute, Andrew. You're on an emotional high. You've had some wine to drink. You just finished dancing. You're feeling euphoric. Let's wait and see what it's like in the morning.*

Well, the next morning the euphoria was gone. I was in just a regular, everyday emotional state. And yet, the calm, confident, deep sense of peace and knowing were still there. I knew I was in love with Regina, I knew I wanted to marry her, and I knew I was going to marry her. Even if she declined at first, I knew I'd convince her eventually. It was part of God's plan.

> **I didn't just think that I knew. I *knew* that I knew.**

I knew this must be the Holy Spirit because I had never before experienced such a strong sense of confidence and boldness in relation to a woman. It wasn't a self-manufactured bravado. It came from outside me, guiding my thoughts, words, and actions in a powerful way. And I sought to maintain an inner silence so I could follow the promptings of this Holy Guide.

Well, I knew the next thing to do was to tell Regina where I stood with her and what my intentions were. But the question was: *Where, when, and how?* I was only going to be at the Domans' for the next three days.

Regina and I spent much of Friday running errands together, talking, and preparing something for Alicia's surprise bridal shower the next day. At one point we were in the kitchen together making a large, elaborate salad for the party. Regina was at the sink washing some vegetables and I was sitting at the kitchen table cutting them up when Alicia unexpectedly returned from shopping and walked into the kitchen.

"What are you doing?" she asked.

Regina said quickly, "Oh, Andrew was telling me about this salad his family likes to eat and asked if we could make it."

I'm sure my face betrayed my confusion, because as Regina kicked at my leg under the table Alicia laughed and said knowingly, "Yeah, right!", and passed out of the kitchen.

Regina and I looked at each other wondering if we had blown the cover for Alicia's surprise party. "I'm so sorry," I said quietly.

"That's okay," Regina said.

Later that evening, Regina and I went for a walk alone together down to a large creek about a mile from their house. It was a pleasant night for November, and the walk down the rugged road overshadowed by ancient oaks seemed like a road to fairyland. We talked about a number of different things: poetry and literature and life. I kept listening and silently asking the Holy Spirit, *Now? Do I tell her now?*, but it never seemed like the right time.

Finally, we arrived at the bridge over the creek. We walked onto it and stood together, looking out at the creek and the black forked trees in shadow. The night air enveloped us with a canopy of brightly shining stars overhead while the water beneath us chattered quietly on its way. We fell silent.

Surely now is the time to tell her, I thought. *Now, Holy Spirit?* Stillness. I knew I only had two days left with Regina, and I had already committed myself to visiting my friend Joe the next day and spending the night. *Now would be a really good time to tell her. I don't know when I'm going to have such a perfect opportunity like this before I leave on Sunday.* Silence. I didn't sense any movement of the Holy Spirit.

After the gentle calm had stretched between us for some minutes, Regina finally said, "Shall we go back?"

On the way back we picked up our conversation again. One thing in particular I remember was this:

"Do you like being a man?" Regina asked. As a writer, she was always trying to get into the heads of her male characters.

"Yes," I said.

"What do you like about it?" she asked.

"I don't know," I said, in what was probably a typical male response. "I just like being a man."

❧

The next morning my friend, Joe McCormick, came to pick me up. I spent an enjoyable day at his house talking and catching up with him. We talked about our mutual friends. Including Beth Morson? I'm not sure. But it is interesting that Joe married Beth within a couple years!

I didn't tell Joe about the new development with Regina nor what I was planning on telling her. I needed to tell *her* first. And I needed to tell her before I left tomorrow to return to Steubenville. Maybe after Joe dropped me off at the Doman's house on Sunday, I could just ask Regina for a brief private talk before I had to leave.

But by early evening at Joe's house I started feeling physically ill—like a cold was coming on. Probably all the late nights and early mornings of the past few days were catching up to me. In any case, Joe noticed and asked if I wanted to go back to the Doman's house so I could get a good night's sleep before my long drive back to Ohio in the morning. I said that would probably be good. In fact, I was so weary that I fell asleep in the car while Joe was driving me the 45 minutes back to the Doman's.

Joe woke me up when we arrived at the Doman's house. After I thanked him and said goodbye, I walked through the door leading to the kitchen, intending to go down to the basement to sleep. But as soon as I stepped through the door I was greeted by a joyful chorus of "Andrew's back!" from a number of people sitting around the kitchen table. Regina was not among them.

"We thought you weren't coming back until tomorrow," Alicia exclaimed.

"Well, I was feeling a little run down so Joe brought me back," I explained.

"Have a glass of wine!" Mrs. Doman, the Italian, said, and poured me a goblet of red wine.

"Thank you," I said. Strangely, all weariness seemed to have left me. I felt fine and joined the group at the table, who were discussing Alicia's bridal shower, which had successfully gone off earlier in the day.

"I was completely surprised!" Alicia told me.

"I thought I gave it all away when you walked in on Regina and me making the salad for the party!" I said. "When I looked so surprised when Regina said she was making my family's special salad for me."

"Oh, no, I didn't guess it was for a shower at all!" Alicia said, "I just thought you had probably mentioned something like that in passing and then Regina kind of seized on it as something to do with

> *It must be obvious to everyone that I'm in love with her. I have to tell her <u>soon</u>.*

you and so started making it; because, you know, when two people are in love they just like to do things together. So I totally wasn't thinking that the salad had anything to do with a surprise party for me."

I smiled; the conversation went on to other topics, but I was only half listening. What were echoing in my mind were Alicia's words, "when two people are in love".

It must be really obvious to everyone here that I'm in love with Regina, I thought. *I <u>really</u> need to speak to her <u>soon</u>.*

A few minutes later Regina came downstairs. She had been sleeping, but her sister Jessica had bounded upstairs excitedly to tell her that I had returned. Regina seemed pleased to see me. She told me she had some friends coming over to watch a film Regina had helped produce at college. I could join them if I wanted.

So later on that evening, I was introduced to Regina's friend, Raquel, and her boyfriend, Chad (now married). Raquel was a striking redhead with an artistic flair. Regina told me that the character of "Rose" in her manuscript was modeled after Raquel, her best friend from school. We talked and watched the movie and hung out together.

As I sat next to Regina during the movie, I briefly considered putting my arm around her, or holding her hand, but I quickly and easily dismissed them. Doing something like that seemed so juvenile, and would probably just confuse Regina, who was probably wondering why I had been so friendly this entire weekend. I needed to speak to her first! I decided I was not going to let this situation turn into one of my cowardly past relationships where I just kind of ambiguously let a young woman know of my feelings for her through quaint non-verbal cues or hiding behind a written letter. No, this time I was going to be direct, telling her exactly what my intentions were in person.

But that presented another dilemma. Could I really tell her that I was in love with her and was planning on marrying her? We had known each other such a short time! Wouldn't she think that I was shallow and impulsive, acting on feelings caused by being thrown together for a few days? And, yet, I knew it wasn't just a fleeting feeling. I knew I was in love with her. I knew I was going to marry her. I *knew* that I knew. I had made the decision and I was totally at peace.

But how could I tell Regina that without scaring her away?

All right, I thought. *I can't tell her I'm planning on marrying her yet. If I did that, she'd probably just scream and run away. So it's too soon for that.*

How about I tell her I'm in love with her? Hmmm. Better, but it sounds a little too certain and shallow. She might get the impression I make a habit of falling in love with girls after spending a weekend together.

What can I say that is true and accurate that won't scare her away or give the wrong impression? Holy Spirit, I need a little help here!

And then it came to me. I would just tell her that I was *falling* in love with her. Yes, that was it. I had fallen in love with her, but I was also continuing to fall in love with her. It was true and it would give the impression of something that had recently begun and was continuing (both true) without giving the impression that it was all wrapped up and I was planning on marrying her next week—which I would have. But there was no need to scare her off with talk like that even if it was true.

Just tell her that I was falling in love with her. Yes. Completely true but not so much information about my plans and intentions that she would run away screaming. Perfect. Now I just needed the perfect time and place to tell her.

5

I tell Regina I'm falling in love with her – and she goes into shock

After the movie, and after Regina's friends had left, I was talking with her in the kitchen. It was late. Again.

"What time does your family go to Sunday Mass?" I asked.

"They usually go to the 10am Mass," she said.

"Oh good," I sighed. "Then I can sleep in a bit."

"Well, actually," Regina said a little awkwardly, "I was wondering if you would be interested in going to an earlier Mass with me and then going out to breakfast afterward."

I was pleasantly surprised. "Sure." *An opportunity to speak to her privately*, I thought. "What time?"

"There's an 8am Mass at Visitation."

"Sounds good," I said.

ॐ∼ॐ

Now that I knew I would have the opportunity to speak to Regina of my intentions, I thought I would sleep soundly that night, given how tired I was. Instead, after going to bed, most of my sleep consisted of hovering between deep slumber and dozing. Finally, around 6:30am, I rolled out of bed in the dim basement. I walked quietly up the stairs to the kitchen.

A sleeping silence filled the house and even the light from the outside seemed to still be dozing. A gentle gray drizzle moistened the air and earth.

I stood at the kitchen sink gazing through the window at the misty morning and reflecting on the developments of the past few days. I don't remember exactly what my thoughts were at that time. I mostly just felt a sense of peace. I knew I was right where God wanted me, doing what God wanted me to do. Being what God wanted me to be—just being still.

A few moments later I heard some quiet movements behind me down the hall.

Regina? I wondered. *No. That would be too weird. It's probably someone else.*

Then I heard the person, whoever it was, walking down the hallway to the kitchen.

Just as I was turning to see who it was, I knew it was Regina.

"Oh! You're awake," she said softly as she came into the kitchen.

"Yeah. I couldn't sleep," I said.

"I couldn't sleep either," she said.

We looked at each other. In the rainy gray light of the kitchen I felt like we were the leads in a B-rated romance movie. *Who wrote this script?*

"Well...do you want to go to the 7:30 AM Mass at St. Eleanor's?" Regina asked.

"Sure," I said.

☙❧

So we went to Mass in the rain. St. Eleanor's was a round, modern church with huge wooden beams holding up the roof. Not many people attended the 7:30 AM Sunday Mass, unsurprisingly, so it was quiet and meditative. During Mass I kept praying things like, *Jesus, please help me love Regina the way you love your bride, the Church. Please help me love her the way you want me to love her. Please help me tell her the way you want me to. Please let me know when to tell her.* Over and over again I prayed this silently in my heart. When I received Jesus in Holy Communion, I prayed even more fervently as I walked back to the pew with Regina. I was not nervous or anxious. Rather, even as I prayed with my whole being, I was at peace and confident—my spirit embracing and embraced by the Holy Spirit.

As Mass ended, Regina whispered to me, "I usually pray a decade of the rosary for my family after Mass. An 'Our Father' for my parents and one 'Hail Mary' for me and each of my brothers and sisters. Would you pray that with me? We can pray for your family too."

"Sure," I said.

So we knelt down and put our heads near each other, whispering the prayers so we didn't disturb the other people around us.

> "**I** suppose it's rather obvious, but I'm falling in love with you."

During the prayers, I kept listening to the Holy Spirit, and knew it was time.

As we finished the prayers for our families, I leaned toward Regina and whispered, "I suppose it's rather obvious, but I'm falling in love with you."

Regina was shocked into silence. Later I was to learn that she was both surprised at learning that I was falling in love with her, and that I had been direct enough to say it. Apparently, she had planned this Mass and breakfast date so she could ask me about my intentions toward her. To her amazement, I had preempted her plan.

As Regina continued to stare ahead and whisper things like, "Wow," I put my open right hand, palm up in her lap. She looked down at it, and then quietly put her hand in mine. She actually did not say a word for several moments.

Then she turned to me and said, "Let's ask for God's blessing on our relationship and His guidance." So we knelt down again and prayed and thanked God for bringing us together and asked Him for grace in our relationship.

We left the Church hand-in-hand and walked through the drizzle to Regina's car. Just before reaching it we stopped, faced each other, and spontaneously embraced. Moments passed. Droplets of water fell from the soft gray sky sprinkling onto the deserted parking lot and trees, enveloping us in a mantel of mist. Still we stood.

Finally, Regina, with her head against my chest, said quietly, "Well, something must be happening, because we're just standing here in the rain."

6

Regina and I discuss our relationship – and inadvertently keep the telephone company and post office in business

Eventually we did get to breakfast. We continued talking about books, writing, and Regina's work with Franciscan friars in the South Bronx of New York City. Regina told me she was trying to practice poverty with them, which explained her plain jumpers and dresses. Every now and then she would pause in the conversation, look at me, shake her head, and say things like, "This is so wild."

As we were driving back to her parents' house Regina asked me, "So, where do we go from here? Where does our relationship go from here?"

Now I knew *exactly* where our relationship was headed, but I was still afraid of scaring Regina away with talk of marriage so soon. Therefore, I was deliberately low-key but perhaps too vague for Regina. I said, "Well, I'm just going to continue to listen to the Holy Spirit and follow His lead."

Regina's heart sank at these words. She had heard this kind of thing before from guys who were trying to sound spiritual but didn't really know what they wanted. They were uncommitted to anything beyond a non-committal dating relationship. (I know that sounds like an oxymoronic description, but it's probably accurate.) Regina was having none of it. She was not going to emotionally invest in a relationship with only some vague illusory hope of life-long commitment. The man must at least be committed, *really committed*, to the possibility of marriage and seriously explore that avenue with her. In a word, Regina wanted courtship; preferably courtship that led to marriage.

At this point Regina was very direct with me.

"Well, you have to take the lead in this relationship. I'm not going to do it. I've done it before—trying to help the man figure out what he wanted—and it just—errrggg....So you have to let me know what you want. I'm coming to Steubenville next weekend for a surprise party for Alicia. So you think about it this week and let me know if you want to date me or not."

In a word, Regina wanted courtship: preferably courtship that led to marriage.

"OK," I said, smiling inside. This was so refreshing for me. It was clear that she wasn't afraid of commitment. And she wanted a relationship that would culminate in marriage—just like me. Already this relationship was like no other one I had experienced before. And I was confident and peaceful.

Back at the Doman house it was time for the Steubenville folks to leave. Regina and I didn't say anything to anyone, or give any non-verbal cues that anything had passed between us. But before I got in the car, I gave Regina a hug and said, "I'll see you next weekend."

Martin and his girlfriend, Charlene, were not returning with us. Later, Regina told me that shortly after we left, she and Charlene were in a bedroom cleaning and Charlene asked Regina what was going on with me. Regina said, "He told me he's falling in love with me."

Charlene yelled, "No way!" and pushed Regina into the closet.

That was their bonding moment. Charlene is now her sister-in-law.

☙❧

In the car, Alicia asked me how I enjoyed the weekend and if I had a good time getting to know Regina. I told her I was falling in love with Regina and that I had said as much to her. Alicia was delighted. I saw her whisper excitedly to Mike; probably something like, "Our plan is working!"

You see, unknown to me, they had been carefully working on getting Regina and me together for some time. Some months ago before Regina and I had first met, Alicia had been telling Mike about Regina's disappointments with the guys she had been dating. And then the conversation had moved to me. Alicia had only met me once but knew that Mike and I were good friends, so she wanted to know more about me. Well, in the midst of Mike telling Alicia about me it suddenly dawned on them, "Regina and Andrew would be great together! Well, we can't tell them. We just have to get them together and then let the Holy Spirit do His work."

This was partially the reason why Mike had asked me to meet Regina in Steubenville; and also why I had been invited to the Domans' for Thanksgiving. Mike and Alicia were very pleased

> **There are three signs to look for in discerning a vocation. All of which I had experienced.**

it was working out so well, but they were discreet about their success, and said nothing to anyone else.

That week I had a confirmation that my relationship with Regina was of God and that it was meant to lead to marriage. A Franciscan friar who was teaching my sacraments class was talking about discerning one's vocation. He said there were three signs to look for.

1. A constant desire for a particular state in life.
2. A *knowing* that you know.
3. A deep sense of peace.

All of which I had experienced. I had desired to be married for years and years even while being open to the possibility of being a priest. And I had just experienced a "knowing that I know" and a deep sense of peace this past weekend with Regina. She was my vocation.

So when Regina and I met again in Steubenville the weekend after Thanksgiving it was just a matter of finding the right time and place to tell her I wanted to date her so that she would know clearly where our relationship was. I say "dating" but really it was courtship. I wanted an exclusive relationship with her where we were soberly exploring the possibility of marriage with each other. We just used the common term of "dating" to refer to it.

Saturday evening after a party for Alicia and a separate party for Mike, we all went out with some other couples to a restaurant in the country. During the course of the evening Regina and I had a chance to take a walk together outside along a dark country road.

"So did you make a decision about what you want in our relationship?" Regina asked.

"Yes. I would like to date you. I would like it to be an exclusive dating relationship. We don't date anyone else," I said firmly.

"Good. Because that's what I want too," Regina replied smiling.

We went on to discuss the logistics of how this long-distance relationship would work with her job in New York City and my studies in Ohio. It started raining again, gently, as we walked, as if to signify, "Everything is going to turn out just fine."

৵৶

This was also the point at which our telephone bills dramatically increased. I would usually call Regina in the evenings after I had some homework done, and we would talk at length. One time we began a telephone conversation around ten o'clock at night and we continued talking until about six the next morning. Some of it would have been rather interesting to listen to. Other parts just consisted of dialogue like,

"I love you."

"I love you too."

"I miss you."

"I miss you too."

All very heartfelt with a depth of meaning to us, but for a third party listening in on the conversation, probably rather dull.

In one of our telephone conversations, I told Regina about how the picture of her in her parent's home had led me to begin thinking that she was a princess who had disguised herself in a plain appearance so that no one would know that she was really a princess. But now I knew the secret – and I was going to marry her before anyone else discovered her. No, wait. I didn't say that part to her yet. But I was probably thinking it!

> She was a princess who had disguised herself with plainness. But now I knew her secret. And I was going to marry her.

The post office got a lot more of our business too. Regina would write me letters the length of small dissertations. I, on the other hand, was already writing papers and essays for school. So though I wrote her at length when I could, my letters to her were rather shorter. Sometimes I even had to resort to postcards signing off with "In haste, your knight in fading blue denim". No shining armor here. All I had was an old jean jacket.

A day or two after Christmas, I drove from my parents' house in Michigan down to the Domans' house in Pennsylvania. After a few days with her family, Regina and I drove to New York City so I could see where she worked and lived in a house for single people in association with the Franciscan Friars of the Renewal.

By the time of Mike and Alicia's wedding on January 8, Regina was thoroughly and obviously in love with me. And I—to Regina's delight—could dance. At the wedding reception, she and I had a wonderful time swing dancing to "It Had to Be You."

Unfortunately, the dancing didn't last long. After the third song, the power in the reception hall abruptly went out. An ice storm was hitting Pennsylvania with uncommon fury, and taken out the power lines. So Mike and Alicia's wedding reception was short – but sweet.

But before that happened Regina's relatives were watching me following her around as she introduced me. It was like a déjà vu experience for them because they had seen something similar happen nearly 25 years earlier at another wedding, when Regina Rusinyak had married Donald Campbell.

The bride's sister, Michele, had introduced her family to a young Marine lieutenant who she had just met in the wedding party: John Doman. Within the year, John and Michele had married. They had named their oldest daughter Regina.

7

Regina and I become engaged — as the result of a misunderstanding

We got engaged as the result of a misunderstanding. After Mike and Alicia's wedding we continued to write and talk frequently with each other despite the distance and our full schedules. The big question on my mind now was; how soon could I propose without making Regina feel rushed?

Toward the end of the 8-hour telephone conversation mentioned earlier which actually took place in early February, Regina asked me if we were "pre-engaged". Not having heard the term before, I asked for an explanation. Regina described it as something between actual engagement and dating exclusively — like "we're going to get married but there hasn't been a proposal yet." Frankly, I think it's a confusing term, but apparently it was in vogue among Regina's circle of friends. I came away from the conversation thinking that Regina was telling me in a roundabout way that she wanted me to propose.

This was not the case.

Yet, during that same conversation Regina suggested that next Sunday I should drive toward New York and she would drive toward Ohio and we could meet half-way at Harrisburg, Pennsylvania and spend the day together. So I was thinking she was trying to give me the opportunity to propose.

Again, this was not the case.

I think this is probably a good example of what can happen when one forgets that when it comes to the opposite sex, girls may do things spontaneously with no other plan or motive, whereas guys usually have a plan or some other motive toward a girl even if their exterior actions appear spontaneous.

So the next day, I called Regina's dad. I had wanted to talk to him in person and ask his blessing to marry his daughter. But because I was under the impression that Regina wanted me to propose when I saw her on Sunday, I had to resort to calling him on the phone. With his characteristic enthusiastic warmth, he told me, "I give you my blessing, Andrew. If you wanted to get married next week, I'd give you my blessing."

What a great father-in-law I have.

৵৵৵

The following Sunday, Regina and I met in Harrisburg, Pennsylvania and went to Mass at Our Lady of Lourdes parish. After Mass we knelt down and prayed the decade of the rosary for our families. As we finished I leaned toward Regina and whispered in her ear, "I suppose it's rather obvious, but will you marry me?"

And again Regina was totally surprised.

"Ohmigosh," she said. "Yes!"

And we prayed for our engagement.

I was surprised that Regina was so surprised and after we left the church and began talking, the misunderstanding about "pre-engagement" came out. But Regina wasn't too concerned about it. She began making plans with me about who should be in our wedding party.

> Regina began to worry that things were moving too fast. I tried hard to be patient.

The only and biggest problem that came from this misunderstanding was agreeing on a wedding date. Since it was February and we were now engaged, I wanted to get married sometime during the approaching summer. But Regina felt that things were moving too fast. She hadn't yet met my parents or many of my bothers and sisters. This situation led to our first major argument.

I knew without a doubt that I wanted to marry Regina and that I was meant to marry her and now that she had agreed to marry me, I wanted to actually marry her (go figure) within a reasonable period of time. Waiting another year and a half to get married after having waited so long just to meet and fall in love with her seemed interminable.

Part of me was trying to be patient and accommodating, but another part of me was screaming to get married. Over the next few weeks the wedding date continued to be a point of contention in our relationship. My spiritual director sided with me and Regina's spiritual director sided with her. My dad sided with me and Regina's mom told her, "Well, you know, your dad and I met and married in less than a year."

"What?" exclaimed Regina. "You never told me that!"

"Well, it's not exactly something you tell your teenage daughter," her mom said. "But you and Andrew are older: you both are mature enough to know what sort of person you want to marry."

I think that was the turning point for Regina.

Finances were a difficulty for me, since with a part-time job, I didn't have much money to bring to the wedding. I knew my friends had spent hundreds of dollars on engagement rings, but Regina assured me that she didn't want something expensive. So before Easter, she came to visit me in Ohio and suggested we look in antique shops for a ring. "I don't mind if it's a ring someone else has worn before," she said. "And I like old jewelry best."

A friend told us about an antique store that might have some old rings, in an out-of-the-way little town in Ohio. We got lost trying to find it, and I was losing patience. Noticing this, Regina said, "Let's just stop and say a prayer that we find an engagement ring right away as soon as we get to the shop." So we did.

We were delighted by the prospect of getting married, but we hated being engaged.

A few miles down the road, we finally spotted the store and hurried inside. When we walked in and asked to see any rings they had, Regina walked right over to the display case, looked down, and saw a delicate silver filigree ring with a tiny diamond in the center.

"That's it," she breathed. "That's the one I want. But how much is it?"

The price was exactly the amount I had in my budget. I put money down for it, and came back before Easter to pay for the rest of it. I took the ring with me to Michigan, where Regina was spending Easter with my family. So after early morning Mass on Easter Sunday at the Carmelite nun's monastery near my parent's home, I asked Regina (again) to be my wife. This time, she was not surprised.

Having the engagement ring and spending time getting to know the rest of my family helped put Regina completely at peace about marrying me that summer. We set the date for August 20, 1994 and bought wedding rings at a Michigan antique shop.

Shortly after Easter, Regina moved to Steubenville so she could be near me for the duration of our engagement. We were delighted at the prospect of getting married, but we hated being engaged. Well, perhaps "hate" is too strong of a word, but generally speaking we did not enjoy being engaged. We felt like runners who were poised to take off at the starting line who were told, "On your mark...Get set...WAIT!"...for several months, with engines revving and gears grinding!

However, we did prepare for marriage by going to Engaged Encounter and Pre-Cana classes. And I went on a silent and solitary retreat the weekend before our wedding. It was then that I composed our marriage consecration prayer that we recited at our wedding ceremony some time after the formal exchange of vows. We renew that consecration once every month on the date of our wedding anniversary.

Regina and I wed — and drive off into the setting sun

I was so thankful when the wedding day finally dawned. I felt like something my whole being had been yearning for my entire life was finally coming to fulfillment after much wandering, prayer, and searching.

I think Regina was feeling something similar. Although she had been involved in planning an elaborate and unique celebration, she was determined that our wedding day be all about the sacrament, not about the details. Like Blanche in *Waking Rose*, on the day of the wedding, she remained in her room and told her sisters, "The only thing I'm doing today is getting dressed and marrying Andrew. If there's any trouble about anything else – the place cards, the favors, the dresses— I don't want to know, so don't tell me. It'll all work out."

And it did.

I came over to Regina's parents' house for a "Veiling of the Bride" ceremony. Regina and I liked the idea of following the Jewish weddings described in Scripture, where the groom comes for the bride, who is ready and waiting for him. Christ constantly uses this metaphor to describe His Second Coming. So we decided that I would come to get Regina from her parent's house and go to the church together. We also discovered that in Jewish tradition, a blessing is prayed over the bridal veil when the groom arrives to take his bride.

So on the morning of our wedding, Regina remained in her room with her maid of honor, praying and singing meditative songs, until I arrived. She had told me to come at an unspecified time, like Christ promised too, but true to my personality, I was early.

> It was as though she had removed her plain disguise to reveal her true identity as a beautiful princess.

When she heard I was there, Regina finally left her room. She came downstairs in her full-skirted wedding dress with a chiffon overlay and a long light blue satin sash with trailing ribbons. It was as though she had removed her plain disguise revealing her true identity as a beautiful princess. After the veiling ceremony we drove over to the church together.

Our wedding was a celebration of life — we had about two dozen people in the wedding party and about 400 guests...plus their children. The Mass was a harmonious blend of traditional and charismatic songs and music with guitars, flutes, piano, harps, and violins. Mr. and Mrs. Nelson did the first reading from the Book of Tobit telling the story of how St. Raphael the archangel brought Tobiah and

Sarah together in marriage after many sufferings and difficulties. The priests commented on how beautiful the Mass was as well as the bridesmaids in their colorful modest dresses designed by Regina.

Franciscan friars were among the priests and servers at the wedding. Father Conrad of the Franciscan Friars of the Renewal presided over the wedding vows. My spiritual director, Father Giles Dimock, gave the homily and the nuptial blessing.

Mary Drennen, the young daughter of Bill and Joan Drennen who are the original models for "Bear" and "Blanche" in Regina's fairy tale novels, was convinced that I and Regina had turned into a prince and princess for real.

The reception was at Cabrini College cafeteria with lots of people, music, food, singing and dancing. Years later the numerous kids that came were still talking about how much fun they had at our wedding.

Some time towards early evening Regina and I changed out of our wedding clothes and disguised ourselves once again as a plain peasant girl and a poor knight in fading blue denim. I then picked Regina up into my arms and carried her through a storm of confetti, cheering people, and balloons as we made our way to my black metal steed (my pick-up truck). After removing the balloons and a potted tree from the cab, we got in, and waving goodbye, drove off into the setting sun.

Epilogue – Happily Ever After

Now, you may be wondering if we lived happily ever after. So far, I would say, yes – at least to quite a degree that one can hope for in this life. But I don't want to give the impression that every moment of our marriage relationship has been bliss without end. That only exists in the next life at the wedding feast in heaven that will last forever and ever.

I was reminded of this reality when on retreat the weekend before I married Regina. The thought came to me that marriage with Regina was not going to fully satisfy my desire for love and happiness — that there was a longing in my heart for a love and happiness which Regina was not capable of giving — nor was any mere human being. Only the Infinite and Eternal Source of all beauty, truth, and goodness could do that. At best, my marriage with Regina would be but a foretaste of the eternal wedding feast that Christ was preparing for those who love Him, where everyone truly does live happily ever after for ever and ever.

Ironically, I think these sobering and deflating expectations I had for our marriage relationship actually helped contribute to its overall high satisfaction and happiness. By being relieved of the pressure of unrealistic expectations, perhaps we were more easily able to forgive each other for our faults and failings.

We've certainly had our share of high-volume, verbal fights, quarrels, and arguments. Given strong personalities like ours, coupled with concupiscence in this fallen world, some of that was perhaps to be expected—even with the help of God's grace. But thankfully, it was God's grace that saved us every time. We made it a point to stay close to the Source of our love through prayer, scripture reading, and the sacraments.

> We've had our share of quarrels and arguments. But thankfully, God's grace saved us every time.

I also made it a point to apologize to Regina each night before we went to bed for any ways in which I had offended her during the day. It became a ritual we did together to make sure we didn't go to bed angry with each other. At the very least we'd call a truce. Sometimes it might take days to work through an issue, but we would pray and talk our way through until we got to the "kiss and make up" part. That was always worth it.

I've read somewhere that a happy marriage is the union of two good forgivers. Marriage certainly is a dying to self for the life of the other.

Another practice I put in place early on in our marriage that contributed to the "happily ever after" experience was the result of trying to manage a full graduate schedule with lots of papers to write while also being married and working 12-18 hours per week. This was a challenge. I had just taken Regina on a date a couple of weeks before. Shortly before that, we had just returned from our honeymoon and I had immediately plunged into graduate school. Of course, I was spending a lot of time studying and preparing papers. And Regina was spending a lot of time alone in the apartment.

One day as I was thinking of all the papers and homework I had due at the end of the week, Regina said something to me like, "When are you going to take me on a date again? We never go out together anymore."

All I could think was, *I just took you out a couple weeks ago and I have four papers due at the end of this week.* And yet, I could see that it was important that we make it a point to spend regular time together as a couple if we expected to stay together as a couple.

Then in a flash of divine inspiration, I thought of our wedding date, August 20. I thought of my schedule, and my planner which had all my various activities written down for each day, week, and month—and I said to Regina, "How about if I schedule us to go out on a date at least once a month on our wedding anniversary—the 20th of each month? Then you won't have to wonder when I'm taking you on a date next, and I'll be able to prepare for it each month because it will be on my schedule."

And we still do this. We don't always exactly hit the 20th each month, but it's usually about then, and we renew our marriage consecration prayer at that time as well.

As a poor college student, I couldn't afford much for dates sometimes, so Regina invented "five-dollar dates." We would go to the grocery store and each of us would pick out a favorite snack for the other, the total of both could not be more than five dollars. Then we would go to a park or the lovely old cemetery in the city of Steubenville, eat our treats, walk, talk, dream, and spend time together.

And nearly fifteen years later, we haven't missed a month. It's just one of the many things we do with each other that help us to live together...happily ever after.

Prayer to St. Raphael for a Wise Choice in a Marriage Partner

Glorious Saint Raphael,
Patron and lover of the young,
I feel the need of calling to you and of pleading for your help. In all confidence I open my heart to you to beg your guidance and assistance in the important task of planning my future. Obtain for me through your intercession the light of God's grace so that I may decide wisely concerning the person who is to be my partner through life. Angel of Happy Meetings, lead us by the hand to find each other. May all our movements be guided by your light and transfigured by your joy. As you led the young Tobias to Sara and opened up a new life of happiness with her to holy marriage, lead me to such a one whom in your angelic wisdom you judge best suited to be united with me in marriage.

Saint Raphael, Loving Patron
of those seeking a marriage partner,
help me in this supreme decision of my life. Find for me as a help-mate in life the person whose character may reflect some of the traits of Jesus and Mary. May he/she be upright, loyal, pure, sincere and noble, so that with united efforts and with chaste and unselfish love we both may strive to perfect ourselves in soul and body, as well as the children it may please God to entrust to our care.

Saint Raphael, Angel of chaste courtship,
bless our friendship and our love that sin may have
no part in it. May our mutual love bind us so
closely that our future home may ever be most like
the home of the Holy Family of Nazareth. Offer
your prayers to God for the both of us and obtain
the blessing of God upon our marriage, as you
were the herald of blessing for the marriage of
Tobias and Sara.

Saint Raphael, Friend of the young,
be my Friend, for I shall always be yours. I desire
ever to invoke you in my needs. To your special
care I entrust the decision I am to make as to my
future husband/wife. Direct me to the person with
whom I can best cooperate in doing God's Holy
Will, with whom I can live in peace, love, and
harmony in this life, and attain to eternal joy in the
next. Amen.

In honor of Saint Raphael:
Our Father...
Hail Mary....
Glory Be....

Our Marriage Consecration Prayer
to the Holy Family

Jesus, Mary and Joseph,

graciously accept us and our marriage which we
dedicate and consecrate to you this day.

Holy Family, we desire to model our marriage and
family life according to your own. Show us how to
be patient and kind in dealing with each other's
shortcomings, for no one is without them. May we
be slow to speak harshly and quick to forgive each
other. Make us true and affectionate, eager to please,
and ready to deny our own will and inclination in
all things, so that we may be of one heart and one
mind in Christ. Help us to imitate your holy life at
Nazareth — to be simple, prayerful, and peace-loving,
helpful to our neighbors, and solicitous about setting
a good example in our community.

Lord Jesus Christ,

grant that both of us may constantly and earnestly
strive to lead a perfect Christian life, so that the
Divine Image of Your mystical union with Holy
Church, imprinted upon us on the happy day of our
marriage, may shine forth more and more clearly.

Mary, Ever-Virgin Mother of Jesus,

we ask through your intercession to be blessed with
holy children. We desire to receive them with love
and gratitude from God as His supreme gift to
marriage, and as a manifestation of our marriage

union. Help us to bring them up in the love and law of Christ as revealed through His Holy Church.

St. Joseph, Foster-Father of our Savior, Guardian of His Holy Mother, head of the Holy Family, assist us by your prayers in all our spiritual and temporal needs. Help us to imitate your great humility and service to our Lord Jesus Christ and His Immaculate Mother. Pray that we may be kept free from being selfish, competitive, or entrapped by material possessions and concerns.

Holy Family, please accept this our act of consecration, and keep the memory of it alive in our hearts each day of our lives, so that we may be found worthy by the help of God's grace, to be taken to heaven, there to be joined by our children forever to praise and thank God with all the holy angels and saints for all eternity.

Amen.

About the Author

Andrew Schmiedicke has been married to Regina Doman since 1994. They have had seven children, and live on a small farm, Shirefeld, near Front Royal, Virginia with assorted chickens, ducks, llamas, sheep, and cats, and occasionally a pig or two. He and two partners own a web development company, Veraprise, and he and Regina run Chesterton Press, which prints Regina's Fairy Tale Novel series and other little books like this one. He also works as a freelance editor with Regina for Sophia Institute Press. Andrew speaks at conferences on marriage, fatherhood, and family life, as well as "Holy Chivalry." He wants to thank the fans of his wife's books on the Fairy Tale Novel Forum (forum.fairytalenovels.com) for inspiring him to write this story down, and he hopes it will encourage all those seeking for their own knight in shining armor or princess in disguise.

Books by Regina Doman:

The Fairy Tale Novel Series

The Shadow of the Bear: A Fairy Tale Retold
Black as Night: A Fairy Tale Retold
Waking Rose: A Fairy Tale Retold
The Midnight Dancers: A Fairy Tale Retold

For children:

Angel in the Waters

For other books, see www.reginadoman.com

LaVergne, TN USA
23 July 2010
190631LV00001B/6/P